Body Langua

C000108000

How To Use Your Own Body Language

To Influence Almost Anybody

By

Curtis Manley

Table of Contents

Introduction

Are you misunderstood?

If you are, it may no bet the words you use but the way you move.

Want to boost your confidence with the skills you already have?

Reading other people's body language is an ability we learn throughout our lives. It's an automatic process as we calculate other's inner thoughts through their nonverbal movements. That's without even knowing we're doing it. Though it does work both ways, others judge us in the same way.

But you can learn how to take control of revealing such clues about your inner thoughts. You can also learn to understand how to read other people's thoughts. Know them better than they know themselves.

Nonverbal language is a silent code. Unlike verbal language, this is a mutual way of communicating across the globe, with only a few variances. If we're aware of this code, the potential for improving our communication skills is endless.

It is true to say that every single one of us has our own set of problems within our lives. These problems are often the stresses that anchor us down. When we feel low, even if we keep it a secret, everyone else knows because we show it in our movements and posture. That forced smile upon our lips may not be reflected in our eyes. This signals to others that we are not being fully truthful.

If you could read a person's thoughts by their movements alone, you could put them at ease and make your conversation more fruitful. I am a lover of life and, for me, there's nothing more satisfying than seeing caring people doing great things for others.

Do you want to be one of those people?

Being able to read body language has many benefits:

- People will trust you more because your movements make you appear confident and decisive.
- As a result of this, you will become more popular and sought after.
- Being needed is a great confidence booster.

What great advantages this could have in your occupation. Or, make sure that you are successful at that next interview.

How?

Because you learned the skills to read the true nature of the person asking you all the questions. That puts you in control. As your communication skills improve, you will ooze with confidence. Sometimes that's enough to be successful.

The next time you're in a business meeting, sit at the table and observe your colleagues. As you do, watch out for unconscious movements:

- How are they seated?
- Who is leaning towards whom?
- Do they fiddle with their hair, or swivel their pens?

By better understanding these nonverbal signals, you will gain an insight into what they're really thinking. You will also put yourself across with more clarity.

Don't delay because knowing the kind of power pose that might get you that next promotion, is a skill worth learning about. Be the one that knows how to read your boss and understand their needs. This gives you the advantage to deliver first.

This is a guide that will show you the way to success!

No money is needed for any of this training, only a commitment to practice what you read. Learn about open and closed gestures and the invasion of body space. Improve your ability to spot a mistruth. It goes even deeper as you get a notion of someone's personality.

Get ahead by knowing when to mirror, when to nod, and when someone is putting up their barriers. What's in a handshake, and what's not?

Tread carefully though! Body language can be a minefield. If you misinterpret you could find yourself in hot water.

Chapter 1 Nonverbal Communication

Secret Code

Imagine you are tasked with creating a computer software program for an Artificial Intelligence (AI) system. Your aim is to teach it to read human body language. Think about where you would begin. Would you focus on the face, hands, legs or even the whole body itself? There is a lot of ground to cover when it comes to focusing on nonverbal language.

Our body language is an intricate code of visual cues known as kinesics. It's something we begin to learn from the moment we start socializing, and then take for granted the rest of our lives. Even domesticated dogs have some understanding of our body language and we of theirs. The unsaid movements of the body are not only a human way of communicating, but many different animals also use it too.

Once you stop and think about language, without words, it's only then that you realize there are a huge number of rules and protocols. Somehow, you have learned them all without ever being taught them. After all, no one teaches us them at school. Yet you know so much.

But, do you know all the unspoken rules and intricacies that are involved in nonverbal language? Even if you did, how do you know for sure that you are translating the unspoken messages correctly?

Game Play

Ever played charades? Of course, you have. It is a popular game played by many. One where you cannot use your voice to express the message you are attempting to communicate.

Most of us will be familiar with the rules:

- You must get across the title of a film, play, TV show or book, to your team, without using any verbal words.
- It's all done by gesticulating signs with your arms and often other parts of your body.

If you watch someone who is attempting to do this, they will also be using their facial expressions a lot more than usual. This could be through the frustration of such a slow way of communicating. In the game, it has slowed down how one can get a message across if it doesn't have verbal language attached to it. It's quite a fun game to play, but one thing it does show is how important verbal language is when using nonverbal communications too.

Now, think about communicating with only your voice no non-verbal language. We do it all the time when we speak on our cell phones. This is a method of communicating whereby you only have half the picture. It's much easier to trick a person when they cannot see your face or your posture. That's probably why telemarketing is so successful. By using keywords, a salesperson might talk us into buying a product that we don't want. Could they have done that so easily had we been in the store talking to them? Maybe they could, but they would have had to work harder at it.

These examples show you the art of communicating with verbal and non-verbal language.

If you meet someone in person, your mind would register what they are wearing without realizing it. If it's an official business meeting and they turn up in casual faded jeans, you might think something was out of place and become wary of them. They haven't even said a word to you yet, but already you are suspicious of them. Yet, if you held a business conversation over a cell phone and the other person was wearing their pajamas, it would have no impact on your thoughts whatsoever.

This shows how intricate nonverbal communication can be. The rules already extend from our gesticulating limbs and facial expressions, to what we are wearing.

Before we embark any further, let's take the three most common gestures that highlight this secret code we are all using.

Four Main Gestures

Smile

Humans are capable of making non-verbal communications warm or cold. Even though temperature is nothing whatsoever to do with how we communicate. Yet, with a lovely smile, we can come across as friendly, helping others to feel a calming warmth. A smile is can put on an amazing show. Not only can it lift your own mood, but studies have shown that it can actually uplift the moods of others. [1] Equally, it is easy to go the other way with an unfriendly scowl, so others may perceive us as cold and hard. Non-verbal communications are powerful enough to change other people's emotions.

When you listen to someone talking, don't you want to listen better if they come over as friendly? This is a happy person who you want to communicate with.

A smile can also reflect your own confidence because others as other people are drawn to you.

We will come back to this topic in our chapter on facial expressions because there is much we can convey in the mere positioning of our lips

Nod

Of course, you should make sure that you're nodding in all the right places in a conversation. If you do it in the right way, it will indicate that you are listening, even if you're not. When listening to someone speaking, most of us will nod because we're tuned into the speaker? This is the type of non-verbal cue that helps to make others feel accepted.

Hand Gestures

It's commonly accepted that if someone crosses their arms, they are fending off the world. Of course, sometimes we sit like that because it's comfortable, so we need to use this stance in the right context. Yet one of the most acceptable postures of wide-open arms can mean "give me a hug," and is embracing to those around you. These are two complete opposite gestures and all performed simply by using our arms. If the arms have such power to alter the emotions of those around you, imagine how powerful that makes your hands. With separate digits, we can utilize our fingers to mean so many different messages.

Most of us understand that a thumb in the air means "okay." Yet raise your middle finger and you are insulting someone. How did this come to be? Who made this stuff up? We'll take a look at hand gestures in more detail later, but the hands can give off some very specific messages.

Attitudes

Already we are building up a picture of how powerful non-verbal communication is. While we're usually conscious of what we say with words, we are not always conscious of what we're saying with our body movements. This is where our attitude may give us away.

For instance, imagine you are talking with a person you don't particularly like. Out of social courtesy, most of us would try not to show this. To some extent, we can role play with words and disguise our dislike for this person. Yet, more often than not, it might be our body gestures that give us away. We may inadvertently stand at a distance, or scowl as we speak with them. All are nonverbal signs that will make the other person uncomfortable. The chances are that if you make them feel uneasy, then they won't like you either.

Whether we're doing this on purpose or not, our attitude speaks volumes when it comes to non-verbal communications. That's why it's important that you take control of your body language, so it doesn't give away your thoughts. Learning how to manage your body language will give you the power to put over whatever message you want.

Now that you have a basic understanding of the power of body language, let's continue on and see what effect this secret code can have upon our lives.

Chapter 2 Facial Expressions

Facial Muscles

There seems to exist an unwritten universal language regarding facial expressions. Charles Darwin was the first to suggest that facial expressions indicating emotion were the same in all cultures. [2]

A theory supported in one study led researchers to the adaptation of six universal facial expressions of emotions:[3]

- Fear
- Anger
- Happiness
- Disgust
- Sadness
- Surprise

Every face is quite unique and lends us a means of individual identity. It's not often that we find our doppelganger unless you are an identical twin.

Although we can often have similar features to other members of our family.

The face is a part of the body that we all focus on when communicating. Eckman argued that the face is capable of more than ten thousand different expressions. That's a high figure when you consider there are only 43 muscles in the human face.

Every change we make in our face will give away our emotions and thoughts, all through nonverbal communication. Facial expressions speak as loud and as expressive as any words you might use.

With the right expression you can make other people feel:

- Fearful
- Happy
- Sad
- Trustful

- At ease
- Confused

These are but a few of the basic emotions that your facial expression can invoke with those you are interacting with. The silent exchange of expression can be as powerful as using the noise of words. Let's break it down a little further to better understand this amazing broadcasting tool.

What's In The Eyes

Oculesics is the study of the eyes used as nonverbal communication. It considers actions such as eye movements, gaze, and eye behavior. The eyes are very expressive and some believe that they communicate more effectively than words alone.

If someone is staring at you, the first thing you will wonder is "why?"

- It might make you a little paranoid wondering if you are doing something unusual or odd.
- Then again, you may wonder if the staring stranger is attracted to you.
- Or perhaps they hold a grudge against you for some reason.
- Could it be that they think they know you?

For sure, they will make you feel uncomfortable because prolonged staring is not acceptable behavior. This is one of the unwritten rules that everyone is aware of.

Your eyes will be busy scanning their facial features searching for other signals:

- Are they smiling?
- Do their brows furrow in a threatening way?
- Are they mocking you?

Within seconds of noticing the unwarranted stare, you

will be busy analyzing all the nonverbal cues. You want to better understand their message to you without embarrassing yourself. What you cannot see, from a distance, is the message conveyed in their eyes. We have very little control over what our pupils are giving away.

Is it true that the eyes are a window to our soul?

What's happening is that the emotions you experience will cause a release of hormonal chemicals within your body. It's not something we have much control over. Someone with a sexual attracted to another should be careful when making eye contact with them. This biological process betrays our personal thoughts through our eyes, by making the pupils dilate. [4]

Eye Brows

Eyebrow style can be a fashionable craze. It often results in females shaving them off, only to draw them back in again. To read the language of the eyebrows though, it doesn't matter whether you have any actual brows or not. It's the two frontalis muscles of the forehead that are sending out all the signals. Though it does make you easier to read if you have brows to help accentuate the message.

Research suggests that eyebrow movement is used more when we use verbal communications. [5] The movement of eyebrows is not always intentional. Most of the time we are unaware that we are using our brow muscles. The study suggests that we use our brows to add visual markers to the tone of our voice. With the position of our eyebrow, as we speak, we are setting the acoustic pitch. Such as if we felt angry then our brows may furrow together. Or, if we ask a question then we may raise our brows, thus setting the pitch for our tone of voice.

Yet, have you ever found yourself moving your brows when you read? We use our brows unconsciously, but it always seems to be in correlation with what we are thinking. Whatever nonverbal message the brows are sending, it's usually in conjunction with other parts of our facial features. Let's take raised eyebrows as an example of conflicting messages:

You may raise your eyebrows if you are asking a question. You are curious and seem to naturally want to raise those forehead muscles. It may even cause your forehead to crinkle a little as your brain is pondering.

Then again, you may raise your eyebrows if you've seen something shocking. In this case, your eyes will be wider.

To understand the nonverbal message, much also

depends on the reaction of the mouth too. For each scenario of our eyebrow images, the mouth will be in a different position.

When asking a question, your mouth may remain closed. There is no further use for your lips until you get the answer. This image is of the lips to questioning eyes above.

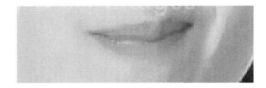

For the shocked look though, the mouth will almost certainly be open. This could be because your breathing pattern has increased. This image is of the lips to the shocked eyes above. Not only is the mouth open but the hands are clasping the face.

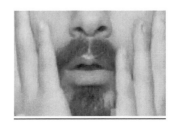

It seems sensible then to accept that our brows, or forehead muscles, work in correlation with the rest of our facial features.

Mouth

This is the most active part of our face. It includes the jaws and teeth that we use to eat and drink. Then there are the lips that we use to smile, frown and kiss. Plus, of course, it includes the tongue that is busy working away when we use verbal communications. That's a lot of muscle action going on in one small place.

How then do we use the mouth in nonverbal communication?

Think about when you are angry with another person. Instincts all over your body will begin to take over, even to the extent that you could be showing your teeth. Okay, you may not be growling, but it's interesting how our lips may part to show those clenched jaws. Does it remind you of a wild animal?

Much the same as a growling dog, you are nonverbally telling the threat to back off. Of course, you will not go all the way and physically bite your offending recipient, unless you are a child. Young children who have not yet learned the niceties of social discourse may well react with such basic instincts. It's not unusual for a child to bite a threatening target. Instead, as an adult, we are more likely to rub the tongue over our teeth with a closed mouth. This bulges up our parts of the face to show our opposition we are not happy with them.

Other parts of the face will be moving in conjunction with the emotion you are feeling. This will enforce the nonverbal message you are sending. We also show our teeth when we laugh, but it's clearly a completely different nonverbal message we're sending out.

The lips can be good tools to use to communicate silent messages without using words. We can make others feel happy, sad or threatened, merely by the movement of our lips. We can blow a kiss in fondness, bite the lip with anxiety, or even compress the lips together in annoyance, all sending out different nonverbal cues.

The interesting one here is the compressing of lips. This is more an internal message to ourselves. When we press our lips together tightly, it usually means we're unsure of something. If you are greeting someone you don't like you may do this to cope with the situation. In a sense, we're stopping ourselves from talking in case we say the wrong thing. Something has unbalanced you or caught you out. Unless you're simply attempting to seal that lipstick you just applied.

Chapter 3 Hands

Tired Or Tense

We have seen how powerful facial expressions are in nonverbal interactions. Body language is not only about our face, it includes the whole body working together. How then do hand gestures fit in with this unspoken code of communication? They are after all the major tools that we use for so many different tasks.

We unconsciously send out messages from the actions of our hands. If someone is biting their nails, it could mean they're nervous about something. Of course, they may be attempting to remove a piece of broken nail. On the whole, though, this gesture indicates anxiety and nervousness. Instead of your nails, you might bite at the end of a pen. It's all the same behavior in that it is the clenching of the teeth as if it brings a sense of relief.

Other hand gestures betray your restless thoughts,

such as tapping your fingers on the table. Or, you may even go to the extent of putting your hands on your hips, all sending messages of angst and anxiety.

The difference between nail biting and hands on the hips is that one gesture is more introvert than the other. Hands on the hips are considered a more confrontational gesture. We unconsciously do this when we attempt to be assertive. In a sense, we're trying to make ourselves look bigger and appear more dominant. How loud the nonverbal message is, depends on the position of the hands and fingers. When at ease the hand will be more spread out and relaxed. Whereas if done threateningly, the fingers will be tighter together, maybe even clenched in a fist.

So many gestures and so many ways to interpret them. Authors Hartland and Tosh (2001) wrote a book titled Guide to Body Language. In it, they claim there are over 700,000 different body movements and postures related to nonverbal communications. That's a lot of interpretations to learn.

With 27 bones, your hands have almost a quarter of all the bones in your body and each hand has over 30 muscles. It stands to reason that we use our hands for more than grasping and feeling, we also use them constantly in our expressions.

Fingers

Our fingers alone can speak many unsaid messages.

Pointing a finger can imply different meanings:

A person may point a finger to show someone directions, trying to be helpful. This pointed finger gesture will be loose and relaxed. The other fingers might make a relaxed loose fist with a relaxed thumb.

Whereas, if a person wants to be confrontational and aggressive, they might point their finger directly at a particular person. The finger will be rigid to enhance the shouting voice. The other fingers will come together in a tighter-fist. Does the pointed finger represent a weapon, such as a gun? It is certainly associated with an angry voice.

Prodding a finger can have a double meaning depending on how you do it:

To prod another person with one finger which stiff and poking hurtfully, signifies aggression.

Yet, to use a few fingers to push gently rather than poke is a less threatening gesture.

Drumming the fingers can send a couple of messages. How it is done can be a tell-tale sign of the drummer's emotions.

To drum the fingertips fast and loud can indicates the drummer is anxious, tense or frustrated.

A more gentle and slower tapping of the fingers can mean the drummer is in a thinking mode.

The thumb alone can also send varying messages.

A loosely clenched fist with a thumb in an upwards position is a sign of agreement or thanks.

If the thumb is in a downwards position it sends a negative message of "no thanks."

Hands

The fingers are busy at work as we use non-verbal communication all day long, as is the rest of the hand. Usually, the hand is only a small part of some intricate nonverbal message.

There will be other body movements going on at the same time, such as:

Hands and Shoulders

With palms facing outward and arms slightly raised, accompanying a shrug of the shoulders. It is a silent way of indicating that you "have no idea," without using any words.

Hands, Knees, Face

Religious people place their palms together in prayer as they kneel down with closed eyes, closed mouth, and a relaxed face.

Hands, Fingers, Face

Waggling the fore-finger to disagree with something. The expression on your face will give away your true emotions on how much you disagree.

Hidden Hands

Putting hands in the pockets could be a form of hiding. The other person cannot read your body language so well, because you're hiding one of the important indicators. Then again, you may simply have cold hands.

The list of gestures with the hands seems almost infinite. Hands are such a crucial communication tool, that humans have even invented sign language by using the hands and fingers. That is a whole new language that does not involve any words whatsoever.

There are other movements to consider in understanding the strength of a hand message. For instance, if someone is performing an insulting gesture with their fingers, are they doing it with one or two hands? By using two hands it increases the vigor of insult twofold, and all without the use of any words.

One Researcher suggests that although scientists believe spoken language evolved from body gestures, there is still a place in modern society for non-verbal communications. Such gestures, he argues, don't only add to the spoken language, they play a fundamental role in it. (6)

Considering we also touch and feel with our hands, it takes the hands to a whole new level, making them tools of intimacy. It's no wonder that we use our hands for our personal communications when they are such an important part of our body.

Chapter 4 Arms

Our limbs also give away many nonverbal messages. How we position our arms and legs can be an indicator of how we might feel about the person before us. For example, we tend to cross arms when we're acting defensively.

Usually, the arms tend to align with whatever actions our hands and fingers are performing. When someone upsets or angers us, our reaction can be to cross our arms, thus placing a protective barrier between us and them. As is often the case with body language, it is a completely subconscious process. It could be that we're attempting to create a barrier when we cross our arms in frustration. Although arm crossing can mean a multitude of things, depending on the environment we find ourselves within.

The message you send when crossing your legs can depend on which continent you live on. In the US, crossing your legs is a relaxed and loose process, whilst in Europe, it is a more precise and formal action. [7]

Let's delve deeper to better understand the sciences of body and limbs in nonverbal communications.

Barrier Or Boredom

As with any body language, you must learn to put those unspoken messages into context with the situation. For instance, if you're crossing your arms while watching TV, this is not because you feel in a defensive mood. Quite the opposite, you're probably relaxed and at ease. It is crucially important when reading body language to also assess the setting of your surroundings.

If you're an entertainer and a large part of the audience have their arms crossed, the likelihood is that you're not very entertaining.

When someone upsets us, we often cross our arms to put up a protective barrier that we don't realize we're doing.

Though, if crossing your arms because you're waiting for something or someone, this is more likely to mean you are bored.

It's not often people place their arms behind their backs. This could be because it's not a very comfortable position. Or, because it leaves the front of your body exposed, making you feel vulnerable. There are some exceptions to this though. Soldiers come to mind when they stop marching, they stand in this way as a part of their drill training. Oddly they call it, "Standing at ease." In this instance, they're following orders and procedures rather than using an unspoken language. But it does show how unusual it is to stand in this way.

People who are more aware of their stance may do this. Soldiers come to mind when they stop marching, they do this as part of their training. In this instance, they're following orders rather than using a language. But it does show how unusual it is to stand in this way.

Those who do stand with their front exposed in this manner, are indicating certain confidence. It could even be considered as an arrogant pose, in that they fear nothing and no-one. Plus, they are quite happy to announce this fact through how they are posing. In this situation, the person will likely hold their hands loosely behind their back, with their shoulders relaxed.

We can convey so many unsaid messages with our arms. Such nonverbal messages can either add to the spoken word or speak volumes without words.

Loud Or Quiet

There seems an instinctual drive that makes us gesticulate with our arms and hands as we communicate. When animals are under attack, they may use appendages to make themselves look bigger. Isn't this what we're doing when we raise up both our arms? We're either conveying a message of how amazing we are, or warning something away, such as a threatening dog. Although this is another instance where the environment is important. You may be waving your arms to catch someone's attention, making yourself look bigger to make sure you're seen.

When the arms are flailing away from the body, we are more or less shouting our message as we try to make ourselves noticed. If we don't wish to be so conspicuous, we tend to keep our arm-talk closer to the body. Consider a shrug of the shoulders. We might even use our hands in conjunction to complete the silent message that we "don't know the answer." This is a gesture held closer to the body, almost as if we don't want to shout out that we don't have the answer.

Most actions will be accompanied by other behaviors. The arm-waving might be performed with closed eyes. This is most certainly a negative behavior and more likely to mean a loud message of, "I don't care." As with all body language, you need to read more than one nonverbal action to decipher the tone and meaning of the message.

Elbows

The joint in our arms also plays its part. If we put our

hands on our hips it's usually an aggressiveness posture. Or, we could be taking a sassy pose to show off a new item of clothing, or encouraging the opposite sex. As the elbows protrude outwards it makes our form look bigger. Chances are that we're expanding our chest out too. Again, that environment is all-important in determining the message.

We can even use our elbows as weapons to enhance our aggressive words. Elbowing people in a crowd to let you through is not a nice gesture, but they do make a good leverage tool with or without words.

Or, we can use them to prop our heads on our hands by leaning the elbows on a table. This would serve to show how relaxed we are without the need for words.

Chapter 5 Legs And Feet

Our primitive ancestors used their legs and feet not only to hunt but also to escape danger. They were instrumental in helping us to survive, and are a major part of our body as a whole. Those who have lost leg(s) can often use prosthetics to help them get around. That's because the use of our legs and feet give us a rich quality in life and a sense of mobility. We need to be able to get around, or we are mighty miserable creatures.

Feet

Basic instincts can have a great influence on how we use our body in nonverbal actions. Notice the position of the feet when you next speak to someone.

Without realizing it, we have an instinctive urge to turn our feet outwards, or away from the other person, if we want to leave the conversation. It could be because we're in a rush and don't want any further delay. Or, we don't particularly care for the person/people before us. The direction of the pointed foot can indicate that is the direction we really want to be moving in.

The opposite is in play if the feet turn towards the other person. This can show the person is comfortable with the conversation. The next someone turns their feet away from you when you speak with them, try standing up, leaning on a wall and cross your legs. This pose creates a sense of relaxation on your part. They may even mimic you by crossing their own legs if indeed they also begin to relax.

Somehow our feet manage to give away far too much information on our inner thoughts. Only if you stop and think about what your feet are instinctively doing, can you control those traitorous signals. The next time you find yourself in an interview or speaking with your bank manager, don't allow your feet to slip under the chair. It's an indicative sign of your lack of confidence.

If you are sat next to someone and their foot is tapping away at a fast pace, it can be quite annoying. Yet, it's also telling you that the person next to you is anxious about something. Mind you, if they've wearing earphone they might be tapping along to the beat of a song, so take into account other things that are going on.

Legs

Seated

The legs are a part of the body that can convey different messages for different genders. Notice how in general, men seat themselves quite openly. Their legs are usually apart, showing a confident stature. You could even read it as the wider the legs, the more brazen their self-confidence. Their position is an exaggeration of the casual. It's almost as if they are putting their sexual status on show, and demanding that you look!

Sometimes men may put one leg up by placing a foot on the other knee. This is another exaggeration of stature by unconsciously making themselves look bigger. Though it is another body posture that displays confidence.

Women though tend to sit with their legs close together. Unless they're wearing trousers, then they may be more relaxed with their posture, but not in as obvious a manner as a man. Is it a silent sexual message women are giving off? By crossing their legs, they are protecting the sexual organs so perhaps that gives the female a sense of security. The way a woman sits with her legs crossed can also give off another silent signal. Much the same as pointed feet, the way she is pointing her knees could signify who she is more comfortable with. Then again, she might just find it a more comfortable position, so be careful and don't overread this posture. Watch out for other nonverbal indicators too.

Whilst men enlarge their position with open legs, women shrink their overall position with crossed legs. Society does tend to preach that men should be large and dangerous, and women should be small and thin. Is it then a cultural influence we have all inherited? It can even be considered effeminate if a man crosses his legs in the same manner as a woman. Then again, if a woman dangles her shoe on and off her foot, beware! It's considered to be an arousing posture and may attract the attention of the men in the room. One wonders how cavemen and women sat when there were no chairs, or shoes for that matter.

Chilled

People who cross their legs when standing, usually indicates that they are comfortable with the situation they are in. They don't feel a need to leave, so the legs and feet are in a more relaxed position.

Ever found yourself standing like this when waiting for a tube or train? Added to your relaxed cross-legged position, you might even lean against a wall. Now you're giving off a message that you're not going anywhere in a hurry.

Tense

When seated, crossed ankles give off a similar message as someone who is biting their lip. It indicates that the person is unsure and feeling tense about the situation around them.

If a female crosses her ankles, she tends to position her

legs to one side of the chair and rest her hands on her knees. Whereas when men cross their ankles, they're more likely to have their legs hidden under the chair. That's because a man sitting so in such a closed and tight position is not the norm. Are they attempting to hide that they're annoyed at something or someone? Look at their hands as these may give a clue to their demeanor. If they're balled in a fist, then they're readying for battle. Perhaps it's a heated meeting.

Torso

As the legs take up quite a portion of the body, they can also force the torso to lean certain ways. This is an added means of reading the nonverbal messages that the legs are giving out. We will look more at this in the next chapter.

Chapter 6 Body Posture

Body Alignment

The way your body align while speaking words, is a powerful tool. Unconsciously it will be sending out nonverbal messages. It can show you if feel relaxed, tense, aggressive or disinterested.

Open

A confident person with a friendly outlook will not show signs of tense body language. Their posture should be open and relaxed with the feet apart and head held high as they look forward. They're not afraid to face the person standing before them.

If seated then they are likely to have their palms open and lean forward as they speak to others. Or may sit in an open and relaxed manner, such as for a man he might open his legs whilst keeping his arms relaxed at the sides.

Closed

As you would guess, this posture is exactly the opposite. Vulnerable parts of the body will be covered in some way. Perhaps arms crossed over the chest. If their arms do hang loose, they will likely cover the groin area.

When seated they may cross their legs or arms. The head may lean downwards with eyes looking at the floor.

If standing they may position themselves side-on when speaking with someone else.

Other signs could be clenched hands, hands covering parts of the face, feet tucked in if seated.

A closed posture will not invite friendliness but rather show disinterest or even hostility.

How the body comes together as a whole, including the head, arms, and legs, will give away those all those revealing nonverbal signals.

Head

The position of a person's heads an important clue as you also attempt to read their facial features.

Are they looking at the floor? They could be shy or not

want to appear confrontational. Or, are they showing signals of boredom from their conversation with you?

The higher a person raises their chin, as they speak, the more confidence they have in themselves. They're not afraid to lift their head up high and make themselves look tall.

A tilt of the head when speaking to someone can reveal all. It could indicate that they find the other person interesting, or at the very least that they are paying attention. People who are not interested in each other will look away quite a lot, as their mind wanders. They may even turn their heads away physically, so their face is not pointed in the other's direction.

Neck

Even the neck will reveal a secret or two as this is where our vulnerable throat lays. When someone fiddles with their own neck it shows they're a little unsure of themselves, so they're loitering near their vulnerable throat. If they're covering the throat then they may be feeling a little exposed. They want to protect themselves from whatever's going on around them. A man may fiddle with his tie, or stroke his chin. A woman might fidget with a necklace, or the neckline of the top they're wearing. All are indicators that they feel uneasy.

The throat itself can give obvious nonverbal signals by how much a person swallows. When anxious people tend to swallow more than usual. Unless we cover up our throat area, other people can read this signal because they can see us gulping.

Trunk

The trunk of the body is much like the pointing feet. If you're comfortable with someone you're more likely to lean towards them, and vice versa. Leaning towards a person is a sign that you are engaging with them. It's a good indicator that you're listening because you're interested in what they have to say.

How your clothing hangs on your body can also be an indicator of your demeanor. If your shirt is open casually at the top, then you're probably feeling relaxed. Whereas buttoned right up to the top can only mean, "Keep out," or "Don't come near me." Much the same as a man's tie, if it's loose then he's relaxing, but he wouldn't wear it like that in the middle of a business meeting.

The trunk of the human body is where the most important vital organs are encased. It's understandable that we're wary of allowing another person close to them. We may keep a distance from someone we don't particularly care for, or know. Only those we trust and love can stand close to those vulnerable organs, such as our heart and lungs.

How we hold our body when we embrace someone can reveal this message better. The closer we allow another person to get to our own body, the more relaxed we are about them. Other silent indicators will be the arms as well. There's the hug that only involves a little pat on the shoulders. At the same time, the bottom halves of the two people will have a distance between them. It usually indicates the two people don't know each other that well. They're hugging as a social nicety.

Then there's the hug of a person you are familiar with, such as a loved one or a long-time friend. In that instance, we tend to wrap our arms tight around the other person's back. The top half of each person's body will touch. We know this person can be trusted so we allow them close without even thinking.

The hips will play a major part in that hug. That's because your genital area is reserved for intimacy. You might allow your spouse or partner's hips to touch your own, but it's unlikely you will allow anyone else in such close proximity, even your offspring.

Consider the complete opposite of a hug. This would

involve turning your back on someone. Is it a coincidence that if we turn our back on someone who we're annoyed with? In a sense, we are protecting our vital organs at the front, and showing them our spine. This body posture is known as ventral denial.

In Eastern cultures, people are more likely to bow the torso to a stranger, than to hug one. Bowing is considered a sign of respect. Yet in Western cultures bowing is only for meeting royalty.

As with the facial expressions, the use of hands, fingers, head, neck, legs, and the sway of the body are all complex. There are so many combinations of movements that it could take a lifetime to learn them all. Given that, it shows it's not simply the pose, but the tone of the pose. For instance, if someone is crossing their arms, what does their face say about their mood. Poses show emotions and they speak loudly about our nonverbal language.

Chapter 7 Can You Trust First Impressions?

When buying property for your home, you will know within the first few seconds of walking through the door if it's the perfect house you're looking for. Can you make such a quick judgment when you first meet a stranger?

Frozen Images

One study published in 2017, [8] exposed subjects to various images of faces for set lengths of time. Each viewing increased in time by milliseconds. They evaluated three traits: trustworthiness, status, and attractiveness. The increase in time made little or no changes to their initial assessments. They had made their first judgments within 33-milliseconds. Most answers remained the same, even when given longer. First impressions imprint upon our brain very fast, but can we trust such a quick judgment?

In determining first impressions we focus on facial

expression and head positioning. A study in 2014, [9] asked subjects to look for certain character traits in different images. The images were of the same people but with different facial expressions. With different head tilts or lighting, the viewers were changing their opinions on the set traits of the same person. The results were indeed affected by very slight changes to the images.

Of course, these frozen images were still. They were of people but they were play-acting. In today's technical world, that's how we see lots of people we don't know. We see strangers every day on our TV screens or through online social platforms. For instance, you may read an article that has an image of a politician who you've never met. According to this second study, you will make your opinion of the person in the image based on how the image was taken. Are they in a dark shadow or sunny light? That might affect your mood of how you perceive them. It might even imprint itself in your brain, to point that's how you perceive that person for the rest of your life.

Yet, we cannot know a person's real personality simply by an image we look at, can we?

Take for instance a dating app. You tend to choose images you find attractive. Then you couple that with the information they provide you on their personality. Then, when you meet up there is a good chance you will be compatible. All you have had though is a still image and you cannot read their body language. Once you meet up this will be added to your opinion of what you feel about your new date. That will be the point of whether your date is successful or not.

Face to Face

An image alone cannot possibly give a correct first impression. You need all those other little nonverbal signals to go along with that face. Even then, can you trust your judgment of a person's character within the first moments of meeting them?

The more knowledgeable you are of your own nonverbal signals, the better chance you have of giving a good first impression. By being in charge of your body language, you are in charge of the messages you give out.

Eye Contact

This is the first and most important visual cue. Practice looking into other people's eyes, even if it's with a loved one to start with. The better you get at it, the more you will exude in confidence. Avoid having a staring contest though, that's will give off a signal of competitiveness. In other words, don't forget to blink and learn when it's good to look away. Don't allow your eyes to flicker around the room. That's going to look as though you're not interested and not listening.

Body Stance

Keep your body in an open and loose position. Avoid crossing any of your limbs so that you're not inadvertently building up those barriers we discussed earlier.

If you find yourself standing and talking to someone who's not responding too well, find a seat. The other person should follow suit. It helps to create a more relaxed atmosphere.

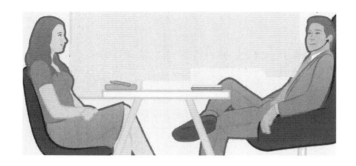

Though if there's not a table between you, try to sit to their side rather than opposite, so it's not too formal. This is so much less confrontational than looking at each other across a table. If you must remain standing, as with the seating arrangement, try to position yourself to the side of the person you are conversing with. Keep your two feet flat and firm to the ground with no swaying around or slouching on one foot.

Be conscious not to fidget with your hands or feet. That may insinuate that you're bored and want to get away as soon as possible. Nod your head occasionally so it appears as though you're listening. It shows that you are committing your time to the conversation.

Think tall and therefore be tall by keeping your head upright, no looking at the floor. Shoulders should be back but not stiff. You don't want to come over as hostile but as relaxed and confident in yourself.

Other Factors

Listen to the tone of your own voice. Don't hesitate in your speech patterns if you can help it, you want to come over as confident. When walking you should do so at a brisk but controlled pace, you don't want to look as though you're rushing.

Research your cultural differences if meeting someone from another ethnic group, for the first time. The most important behavior of all is not to forget to smile.

Remember, the chances are that other people have already assessed you before you even get to say your first word. Though it does work both ways, so you will have evaluated them too. Take this into account and tell yourself that you need to get to know them better before cementing your first impression.

It is in our nature to go by first impressions, and that happens within the first 30-seconds. In fact, we make our first impressions before we even say a single word. The instinct of fight or flight plays out subconsciously. Our mind is busy considering a multitude of possibilities. "Can we trust this person? Are they a threat to me? I don't like how he's looking at me, so I don't think I like him?"

It seems unfair to do such an important assessment in this way. Yet the science is there to prove this is exactly how we behave. No doubt, if the person is in our lives for longer, our conscious thoughts can override our split-second decisions. After a few meetings, we might start liking them better as we get to know their true personality. Unless you're good at controlling this form of nonverbal observation, it shows how easy it can be to make enemies.

Chapter 8 Comfort Versus Discomfort

Bad Habits Are Infectious

Have you ever become aware all of a sudden, of some bad habit you're acting out in a silent room filled with other people? It could be something that doesn't normally stand out, such as shuffling your bottom in your chair.

It's a sure sign that you're not comfortable with the situation you have found yourself in. You want out as soon as possible. We can all be guilty of displaying anxious habits when we're in a situation that makes us feel as if we don't belong.

The secret is to recognize such habits and stop them from playing out. That way you are not subconsciously disclosing any signals about your inner thoughts. Otherwise, you might never get invited back to that big meeting again. All because you're known to distract people as you shuffle around in your chair, or whatever it is you do. It is a little like the yawn, if one person does it, others will follow. No one wants a person who distracts them when they're trying to concentrate. You might end up with no one sitting next to you.

Then, it comes to your turn to have your say in the meeting. Without realizing it, you end up fiddling with your sleeve or coughing into a clenched fist. All indicators that you lack confidence. Such nonverbal movements make you look nervous and will unsettle your audience. That's why you must take charged and think on your feet.

How have we come to the understanding of what is considered uncomfortable behavior? It's not something we learned at school because body language is not on any curriculum. It's one of those social skills we've learned through personal experience. Somehow, we know that it's not polite to stare. It's considered a negative nonverbal signal and unless we want trouble, we don't do it. This gesture has a similar result as pointing a finger at someone. By picking them out you're more or less accusing them of something, and they will not thank you for it.

Most of us want to appear confident. We want to look welcoming on the outside. That makes it important to recognize when you're making other people feel uncomfortable. It's a good skill to discern when other people are feeling uneasy. Only then can you can help them to relax, particularly if you work with members of the public.

Personal Space

One unwritten rule we have not yet discussed is that of personal space. Folding arms across your torso may be an attempt to build a barrier, but it doesn't always mean that others will comply. Most especially if you're in an aggressive scenario. It's one time when we purposely stand close to our opponent, usually in an attempt to intimidate. Our defensive/aggressive traits are forcing us to look tough, even if we're shivering wrecks inside. It's an important social nicety to understand another's personal space. Stand too close and they may assume that you're on the attack.

Nobody likes a stranger to behave oddly. When confronted with unacceptable behavior, we tend to move away from the offending person. In a sense, they worry us. We assume they're about to do or say something detrimental. Why else would they seek such attention? If they're not behaving friendly, we may view them as our enemy.

Sure, we've all been in a situation where we're packed like sardines trying to get into an NFL match, or on the subway, or train. We tolerate this situation of touching shoulders with people we don't know. We won't look them in the eye to confront them because it's an acceptable situation. They are not our enemy because they are in our personal space. It isn't something we particularly like though. You would not touch a stranger unless there was a good reason to do so. What then is this unspoken rule of space?

The study of personal space even has its own label, it's known as Proxemics. On average our personal area can radiate out between 1-5-feet. This is our little bubble where we don't want anyone, other than people we trust, to step any closer. It's our comfort zone. A place where we don't want strangers entering without some agreement from us that they can do so. Personal space is not only about a physical area of space, but it also includes things that trigger our annoyance.

Invasion Of Personal Space

This first one is a true invasion of your inner comfort zone. How do you feel about strangers touching you to search your body, such as at an airport? We all find it an uncomfortable experience. It is, of course, a perfectly legal procedure but it is still personally intrusive.

How annoying are people who talk loudly into their cellphones as if there is no one else around but them? Much the same as neighbors who play loud music at unsocial hours.

Then there's the cold callers who knock on your door or constantly ring your phone number.

Let's not forget the drivers who come right up to your rear fender. They might as well attach a tow-line and come along for the ride. Not only is it invading your space, but it's also dangerous.

Other invasive behaviors could be cars polluting your street because they insist on taking a short cut. Someone jumping a queue. Someone wearing a perfume that makes you sneeze, and so on and so on. It's never-ending how much we all have to put up with each other, and all without speaking a word. The more anxious your nature, the larger your personal space will be.

In the 1960s, anthropologist Edward Hall summarized that in our mind's eye, we have four different unseen personal zones:[10]

- **Intimate Space** is around 18 inches from our body. It is for loved ones, close friends and pets.
- **Personal Space** can be 1.5-4-feet away from our body. We will converse with casual friends or work colleagues comfortably, so long as they adhere to this distance.
- **Social Space** can go as far as 4-12-feet away from our body. We're okay with strangers appearing in this zone, once we've assessed them from the furthest zone and allowed them to get nearer.

- **Public Space** can be 12-feet and beyond. This is where we first begin to assess strangers. For most of the time, we will ignore people in this space, unless they wish to enter our Social Space.

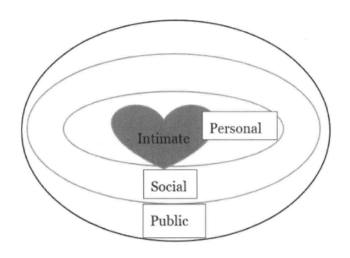

Other factors are also at play, such as gender, culture, and personality traits, when measuring the effects of personal space. The vast research is showing that it is difficult to measure nonverbal behavior. Daphne et al [10] undertook to measure brain activity in correlation with personal space. [11] It showed there is more activity in certain parts of the brain when another person comes too close than when an object such as a moving car, comes close.

Other research shows that personal space may be an innate behavior we inherited from our primitive ancestors. Many wild animals and insects show signs of personal space behaviors. A dog may bark when a stranger enters its territory. Ants attack when other insects stray too close to their nest. Personal space could be a survival mechanism in its raw form.

Personal space is important to our territorial space. Consider the situation where you have to attend a business meeting. Don't you feel that it's to your advantage if it's held in your own building? It's a kind of "home-field advantage." Going to the other person's home turf makes you feel at a disadvantage. Whilst it's not our personal space, it is in our own territory. Think of a soccer match, your team has a better chance of winning if they play in their home ground, or so we like to believe. We need to adopt certain skills if we are to perform away from our home-field.

When we take a seat in a busy room full of people, we tend to leave an empty chair between ourselves and the next person, if we can. Or we try not to sit next to someone on a train or bus if we can avoid it. Somehow, we need to set that buffer zone for our interpersonal distance.

It's much the same in a business meeting; the table should have dynamic seating arrangements if the meeting is to be successful. There should be no gaps at a business table as people need to bunch up so they can hear one another. If you're clever with your seating plan you might arrange to place an influencing character among the quieter ones. This might encourage the meeker speakers to contribute more.

Neural signals in the brain react to the nonverbal movements playing out around us, wherever we are. Such unsaid actions are great influencing factors to whether we feel comfortable with one another, or not.

To measure the right space though, can change according to the situation, such as:

- Those who live in a city may have a smaller personal space than those who live in the open country. Inner-city life is busier and faster and people need to adapt to their surroundings.

- The more anxious a person is, the more personal space they need.

- One interesting gender difference is that men usually need a larger space from other men. Yet women generally don't need that much space and feel comfortable being close to other women. Mix the two and women will want a bigger gap from a man, but men will want a smaller gap from a woman.

How you stop someone from entering your personal space is not an easy task. Being more aware of nonverbal language means you'll be better at predicting other people's thoughts and movements.

For instance, if you know someone's a hugger, stick out your hand for shaking before they get the chance to open up their arms and give you a huge bear-hug.

As with most topics in life, the more you understand, the better you will become in finding coping strategies. What do you do though if someone is purposely misleading you? Can you tell in their body language?

Chapter 9 Misleading Nonverbal Actions

How To Spot Mistruths In Nonverbal Signals

We are none of us perfect. Many of us will be happy to mislead others into believing a mistruth, or rather an outright "lie." Even those of us considered to be "honest" people can be tempted to tell the odd "lie," if the situation needs it.

It's not always easy to interpret if someone is attempting to mislead you through the words they speak. You can attempt to get ahead of their game with the help of their nonverbal actions. Tread carefully though, for all may not be what it seems.

Mouth

Let's take the simple gesture of a smile. A smile usually brings warmth and a feeling of relaxation to the recipient. There's a name for a real smile, which is a Duchenne smile. It should include the crow's feet crinkling around the eyes and the corners of the mouth turning up.

But we are capable of fake smiling so we can look as though we're being honest and friendly, even if we're not:

- We may raise a false smile if we're attempting to be brave, to mislead others and maybe even ourselves.
- When being interviewed we try to smile but inside feel anxious and nervous. Again, we are misleading others.

Eyes

The eyes can give away a person's intentions, in much the same way as the smile we discussed earlier:

- Some people have difficulty looking others in the eye when they're attempting to mislead them. Their eyes may flick around the room not focusing on anything in particular, or stare at the floor in a fixated manner.

- Others though can manage to out-right stare all the more, almost as if they're daring you to accuse them of lying.
- They may attempt to look you in the eye but blink faster than normal.
- None are much help unless you know the normal characteristics of a person's body language. Although all these actions might spark a flicker in your brain that something is amiss.

Hands

Other indicators of what you're really feeling can be given away in your hands.

- Someone who feels uneasy may fidget with their clothing or accessories, as they feel a need to move their fingers around.

- Or, they may tap incessantly, playing out their inner anxious feelings.
- Some may feel a need to cover their face and fidget with their chin, or scratch at their nose. It's a sort of self-shaming process.
- Then again, they could simply raise that barrier between themselves and whoever they're lying to, by crossing their arms or legs. [12]

Personal Space

Someone who knows they're not telling the truth may either stand too close or stand too far to keep their distance.

Despite all these nonverbal signals, it can still be confusing to capture warning signs. They're easier to read when you know the other person's normal nonverbal behavior. If it's someone you're not too familiar with, you could easily misread such nonverbal actions. They are all possible indicators of anxiety. When someone attempts to deceive, they often feel anxious. Then again, there could be other legitimate reasons for them to be feeling such emotions. It is a fine line.

One study explains that a deceiver must face the challenges of hiding their own guilt or shame. [13] If indeed they feel such emotions then it will lead to nonverbal cues. This particular study indicates that these cues are more likely to play out in the feet and legs. A little less in the hands and even less in the face. It seems upside down but it is because people are more conscious about their facial expressions. Particularly when lying. They're unlikely to think about what their legs are doing so this could be the key factor, the true give away sign.

Non-verbal communications are more complicated when the person you are studying is able to conceal their true emotions. It means they can send out deceptive non-verbal signals. A study published in 2018 indicates that we are more able to detect deceptive negative emotions, than positive ones. [14] Having the ability to fool others on which emotions you non-verbally show, is the answer on whether your lying is successful or not.

People, on the whole, don't expect to be lied to. We automatically believe something we're told unless there's a sign to trigger otherwise.

Stance

Some liars can hide their lies in nonverbal actions by standing in a rather stiff manner. They purposely keep their body stiff so they don't give away any emotions in their actions. Yet, if a person is doing no non-verbal cues, it's not a natural stance to have. That in itself should be the key warning that triggers our senses.

There have been many studies and much research on the topic of fully understanding nonverbal signals. Yet still, there are no clear-cut answers because it all involves human emotions, which are not very reliable.

One such research indicated that when we tell lies it automatically triggers a complex cognitive process in our brain. It stands to reasons that lying can be mentally taxing. The speaker will be working hard to hide any telltale signs. Most scientific studies conclude that it's easier to tell if someone is lying from verbal clues rather than nonverbal ones.

Researchers looking to assist law enforcement have published their results for Forensic Psychiatry. [15] They expressed that training is needed so as not to over-analyze the nonverbal observations when someone is lying.

There are usually more verbal than nonverbal cues that are better reliable:

- The speaker may be vague about certain details that they're describing. They don't seem clear on what they're talking about. When confronted about their confusion, they can either pretend not to know or refuse to continue the discussion.

- If they speak fast or appear confused with their speech, it's another verbal indicator that something is not quite right. For instance, they may repeat words as they appear flustered. They may also oversell their tale, repeating a scene that is almost rehearsed. All sure signs that should ring alarm bells.

- When confronted with specific details, the speaker may well attempt to shrug off the answer. If challenged on this, they may begin flustering with their nonverbal actions, such as shuffling feet or fidgeting hands. They're attempting to hide their emotions so as not to give anything away.

Nonverbal messages can be misrepresented i.e. they could be actions reflecting emotions for other reasons. We cannot assume that everyone who shows anxiety through their body language is telling a lie. Are they crossing their arms because they feel cold?

When someone says they feel fine and smiles, but you know they are suffering, you are picking up mixed signals. A good communicator will learn to recognize these conflicting actions, such as when nonverbal signals don't match the situation.

Chapter 10 Conflicting Gestures And Stress

We do need words to communicate with one another, but that is only part of the picture.

Professor of Psychology, Albert Mehrabian, developed a theory called the 7-38-55 communication rule. This encompasses the belief that 7% of our communication is with words, 38% is our tone of voice and the remaining 55% is based on our nonverbal signals. [16]

Much of what we say is judged by our actions, and most of the time, those actions will match the words. What does it mean then if someone uses words that simply don't match their nonverbal signals?

When this happens, we may get a "gut" feeling that something isn't quite right with what a person is saying. Subconsciously, we've recognized that their body language isn't matching their verbal language.

Now we become suspicious as our senses tell us something is amiss.

Case Scenario

Take for example someone who says they agree with a suggestion you have put forward at a meeting. As they say those words of agreement, they also roll their eyes and turn their head away from you. It is the eye gesture that is the nonverbal action showing conflict to their words. You know by this silent action that they are not being honest with you. They also seem to have an internal uncertainty on how to handle the situation. Had they not rolled their eyes you would have had no idea they did not agree with your suggestion.

This is a good example of someone's body language

being incongruent with their verbal communication. When we notice conflicting micro-expressions, we are more influenced by the nonverbal cues than the words the person is speaking.

As we have previously discussed, it is very easy to misread nonverbal signals. You may read too much into an eye-rolling gesture. That's why you need to look out for other nonverbal gestures that will support any evidence that this person is not being honest with you. In our example scenario, the person also turned their head away as they rolled their eyes. This is a classic sign of disagreement and also a lack of respect. It is as if they are turning away to laugh at you as they used their misleading words. When seeing more than one conflicting nonverbal action, you are right to be suspicious. Their own body gestures gave away their treachery. This is how you can determine what weight to give those body gestures. Look at their overall outward demeanor and not only one movement.

If you are sure they disagree with you, one way to deal with their conflicting message is to confront them. Not in an aggressive way but to calmly ask them further questions. Each question attempting to get to the truth by words or by body movements. Though be careful, let them see that you're asking for clarity, not questioning their motives. This will encourage further debate and help you can get to the bottom of why they rolled their eyes, yet said they agreed with you.

Diplomatic skills will be required. By confronting their hidden agenda, you may cause them alarm. To get to the truth of the matter, show that their opinion and contributions are important to the final outcome. This is where utilizing your own body language could be important. It is you who is now doing the confronting, so learn how to do it without raising their shackles.

Nonverbal language does delve deeply into our emotions. If we can control our own stress levels, can we then learn to give off more accurate body language?

It is possible to regulate what messages you give away through the movements of your body. Understanding neuroscience will give you a helping hand.

To improve your communication skills, it's about giving off fewer nonverbal cues and picking up on other people's secret movements. If you can do this when there is obvious conflict, you can learn to diffuse situations before they get out of hand.

To help in this, it's important to understand how to control certain automatic body reactions, such as:

- Patterns of breathing.
- Blushing cheeks.
- Sweating brow.
- Excessive swallowing.

By controlling any of the above bodily reactions, you will give off fewer nonverbal secrets of your inner emotions.

What then of our personality traits? If we are natural worriers, can we never learn how to control our movements in a confident manner? Are these the key to controlling our nonverbal actions? This is an interesting notion, and if it is true, should we try to change our personality?

Chapter 11 Does Personality Drive Body Language?

We have seen how much our emotions can rule our nonverbal actions, but how much are we giving away about our own personality traits? These are the forces that make us an individual character. Does our nonverbal body language really give away too many secrets?

Personality Development

What then is our personality and how can we protect it from being so publicly open?

According to a study in 2007, there are five main personality traits known as "Temperament Traits." These are: [17]

1. Shyness to Boldness
2. Exploration of Avoidance
3. Activity to Laziness

4. Sociability levels

5. Aggressiveness

Each trait was measured on a sliding scale at a young age. Then measured again when a little older. The results were indeed different.

It means that our personality is a dynamic construct that can alter our life experiences.

One of the founding psychologists in the discovery of personality traits believed that personality was linked to the body's movements. [18]

He identified three main traits of a person's personality:

- Behavior is referred to as the **Cardinal** trait. This is what drives us, our desires and passions.
- The **Central** trait is not as dominant as Cardinal traits but still helps to develop our personality and

behavior. These traits tend to be universal. A typical Central trait could be that you are "hard-working".

- The **Secondary** trait is not always apparent. They only present themselves in certain situations. For example, you might normally be an easy-going person, yet you lose your cool when driving the car.

The book continues to explain that our personality traits are revealed in how we move. We give off clues in our everyday movements, such as how large or small our walking stride is.

Examples of this can be compared in the movements of introverts and extroverts:

- **Extroverts** will be more open in their usage of body language. They have no fear of looking directly into the eyes of anyone they speak with.
- **Introverts** tend to keep their arms closer to the body with closed gestures when speaking. They will be reluctant to look into another person's eyes.

That's because of their lack of confidence and shyness.

Can Personality Change In The Course Of Life?

Case Scenario:

Jayne is a fictional character.

She is a shy and introvert teenager who was bullied at school. Her stepfather was not supportive or loving. He laughed at how she buried her head in books. Her mother was quiet and unassuming, and Jayne witnessed her beatings.

We have a typically shy person from a poor and abusive background. No one thought she would ever be successful. She would most likely work at a store filling shelves all her life.

Jayne felt as if her childhood would never end. To blank it out she studied hard so she could forget how awful life was at home. She worked hard to get good grades, not that her parents cared one way or the other.

All anyone ever thought of Jayne was that she was a shy retiring person, showing very little in regards to a positive personality.

Her hard work at studying resulted in achieving good grades. She worked all hard to gain a scholarship. This meant she could go to college and leave home. Finally, her personality blossomed. She didn't have many friends but the ones she did have were special to her. They studied together and worked hard. She never returned home and went on to be successful with her career choice. As an adult she was confident and a force to be reckoned with. Her shy personality grew and matured to shape her into a completely different person.

This tale is an example, albeit a fictional one, of how our personality can change over a lifetime. There are many Jaynes, or even Johns, out there, who manage to forge ahead in life and change their personality regardless of their background. Many research studies predict bad outcomes for those from a stressful and abusive childhood. This does not mean it will happen to everyone who comes from an unprivileged background. Beliefs can be changed as we blossom and grow.

Many studies indicate that our personality is molded by the time we ware around 3-years old. To some extent, certain traits may well remain the same throughout our life. Some though can change as we develop and learn. For example, let's assume that our shy Jayne used very closed body language as a child. She was introverts and shy after all. Then as an adult who was able to make her own decisions, she became more confident. Her whole outlook on life was altered with her new sense of freedom. Jayne had the right mental attitude to do well as an adult, but as a child, she had no control over her life. Whoever says that personality never changes must think that the human race is made up of robots.

By judging a person's body language on what we perceive as their personality, may cause us to arrive at the wrong assumption. If we categorize everyone, such as assuming that all shy people will behave in exactly the same way, we are acting judgmental. It would make things easier if this were the case. Then again, it would also mean the human race lacks individuality and personality. Just because someone blushes does not mean they're guilty of something. It could simply mean they're embarrassed, or maybe too warm.

Most of the people we meet in our everyday lives are people we either don't know too well, or they're complete strangers. Considering this, you can't judge a person's personality by whether or not they cross their arms.

If it isn't our personality that subconsciously dictates our nonverbal actions, then what is it?

Well, there are a few influencing factors. How our mind operates is a strong influence on our nonverbal signals. Our mind can only assess things on what we have learned. In this, education will have a strong bearing. Although we know that subconsciously our mood and emotions are the stimuli to our body movements, by controlling our emotions it might help us alter our nonverbal signals.

You cannot read correctly the moods and emotions of a stranger. Though you are better able to understand someone you are familiar with, such as friends and loved ones, because you already know their habits.

Indeed, reading someone's body language is a complex skill. To make it even more difficult there are even further differences added to this process, such as gender and culture.

Chapter 12 Universal Body Language

Most countries have different spoken languages as we move around the world. So too the body language changes, depending on whom we're speaking with. To complicate this secret coding even further, it's not only affected by cultural differences, but also by gender differences too.

Gender

In the past, and to some extent even now, sales have been a very male-oriented career. Surveys have indicated that women influence around 80% of household spending. Yet, in most cases, the salesperson they're likely to speak when purchasing for the home, with will be men. Though the present trend is seeking more equality across the career spectrum. One study looked at the different tactics in gender body language in this area. Here are a couple of the observations made in this study. [19]

Female sales personnel tend to smile and nod more than men. They use these actions to help them build up a sales relationship with their clients. It's not only in sales scenarios where this happens. Women, in general, tend to nod and smile during any conversation, much more than men do.

Male sales personnel used eye contact more often than women do. Men use this action as they attempt to dominate the clientele relationship.

The study went on to show further differences in typical gender nonverbal stances. It highlighted how messages can be misinterpreted when the sale is pitched to a member of the opposite sex:

- Female sales personnel tend to build up a friendly rapport in the first instance. They believe this is the first influencing factor to lead to a successful sale. Their actions may include nodding and smiling. Yet, such non-verbal gestures to a male client mean an agreement has been concluded.
- If a male salesperson uses eye contact with a female client, they could make her feel uneasy. Yet, this is a typical stance of male sales personnel.

These are only two examples of how gender body language can send the wrong message when used on the opposite gender.

It's not only the message we are sending but also how we send it. For example, a man usually offers a firm handshake in greeting. Whereby a woman may only offer her fingers in a handshake. Yet another example of gender nonverbal communication differences. If a man only offered his fingers, he might be considered effeminate. Wow! It shows the strong statements we make when using nonverbal communications.

What these observations can tell us is just how complex the secret code of body movements can be. Nonverbal communication is used in different ways by each gender set. It also appears to send out different messages to the opposite sex.

In a world where you must be careful what you say verbally, in case you insult someone, what implications does this have on nonverbal messages?

Cultural

Let's take another instance where nonverbal communications may be misread. This time it's not by gender differences but by cultural contrasts.

It is possible to travel the world without the ability to speak any other language other than your own. The same cannot be said for nonverbal communications. By making what you might consider a friendly gesture, in some cultures that movement may be an insult. For example, some cultures point with their thumb. They would be most insulted if you used your finger for pointing.

Does this imply that body movements are actually more powerful than verbal language?

The differences in cultural nonverbal communications are often based on gender differences too. An interesting result of an anthological study on Proxemic Behavior highlighted this point. The research showed how Arabs interact much closer and gaze longer at their partners than Americans do. The study identified some cultures as more "close contact" friendly than others. This included nonverbal communications such as physical touch and private space. For instance, Arab males sit closer to other males than American males do. [20] It reflects once again the gender nonverbal differences

Charles Darwin was the first to suggest that the facial expression of emotion was universal. [21] This was supported by a study in 1971. It was agreed that there are six universal facial expressions of emotions that remain the same across cultures.

These were:

- Fear
- Anger
- Happiness
- Disgust
- Sadness
- Surprise

Studies show that a person can alter their nonverbal actions as they move through cultures.

James and Jane are American. They have gone to live in Canada. Many of their neighbors are American so they continue to use the same style of body movements when communicating with them. This changes though when they communicate with the Canadian people they are living among.

People can adjust their unspoken movements according to culture when it is necessary to do so.

Interpretation Of Nonverbal Differences

Does it come down to how we perceive another's nonverbal gestures or is it more powerful than that?

For most of us, it is true to say that we don't even think about how we are interpreting body language. Unless you come across a guide such as this one, or a media article on the topic. You are unlikely to go around thinking about how you're reading a person's body language. Yet you are doing it all the time, all be it automatically. The people around have similar nonverbal techniques as yourself. There's little chance that you would interpret their messages wrong, even with strangers from your own culture. Only if the other person showed insult at your gesture would you then think about what you had done.

Given how automatic this skill is in our lives, imagine how powerful a tool it is for someone who is manipulative. It's been proven in the art of Sales that you can clinch that deal with the right nonverbal techniques. If you learn to manipulate others by using nonverbal communications, it would certainly lend you an advantage. Just as you can tell lies with verbal words, so too could you mislead others with nonverbal movements.

Why would anyone wish to do this?

Well, it could reap rewards such as:

- Communicating more effectively could lead to advancing your career prospects.
- Boost your self-esteem, by learning power poses using nonverbal actions.
- Increase your popularity, by learning to show how interested you are in listening.
- Get others to agree with you more often, by eliminating nonverbal barriers and being more open.
- Learn how to make others feel better about themselves, by stimulating their mood with smiles and open gestures.
- Learn to recognize the truth from a mistruth, by watching for conflicting nonverbal movements
- Exude in confidence simply because you're sending out the right nonverbal cues.

Learn to do all these positive actions without using one word. Though it's important to make sure your verbal communications match your body language. If it doesn't, people will notice and you may only succeed in creating confusion. It's not a skill that will come naturally, it will take some learning. To use nonverbal language to your own advantage, you need to understand nonverbal messages in the first place.

To do this, you should do lots of research and teach yourself the nonverbal language of the cultures that surround you.

Chapter 13 Mimicking Behavior

Putting People At Ease

When someone greets you with a smile, it's polite to smile back at them. The smile is an unspoken gesture that helps put people at ease. When we smile, we're announcing that we are not a threat to anyone. To smile yourself, or to see someone else smile at you, helps to release those feel-good hormones of endorphins and serotonin. That, in turn, helps to lower blood pressure, so it's a very healthy gesture to perform or to receive. It is certainly one of those gestures that does not require words and is very infectious.

When someone smiles at you and you return it, by mirroring their gesture you are showing them that you understand how they feel. You are also indicating that you feel the same way. This is only one small example of how we use nonverbal gestures to communicate with one another. It's not something we do intentionally. When we mirror a smile in the right situation it helps to build up trust. Each understands that both are on the same wavelength. In turn, they will feel they can have a rapport with one another.

A study in 2017 indicated that women tend to smile more than men. [22], Men are more likely to express annoyance in their facial expressions. It showed that men prefer to mirror other body gestures that don't involve the face so much.

Synchronization In Romance

Romantic relationships often involve two people who are in rapport with one another. When sexually attracted they may not realize how much they mimic each other's actions. A woman may twirl hair through her fingers. She is in an excited, yet anxious, moment as she speaks with a man she feels attracted to. In response, the man may pull at his ear, or run his fingers through his hair. He is fidgeting with his fingers as he mirrors her actions. Subconsciously, he's observing her every move. These two people are in-tune with one another.

Mirroring someone in a conversation is a form of micro-gestures. They help to put people in sync with one another. It can be seen happening in many parts of the body, such as:

- Blinking at the same time.
- Raising eyebrows at one another.
- The Crossing of arms or legs.

The Trust Of A Friend

Friends and loved ones tend to mirror one another's body movements the most. They have no hang-ups with each other's presence. That's because they've learned to trust each other over the years. But, they're not the only ones that do mirroring naturally.

Seeking A Promotion

Let's take those who are looking to move up the corporate ladder. In their keenness to impress the boss, they'll most likely inadvertently mirror the body movements of their superiors. They want to get the message across that they have similar points of view and respect the person they're mirroring. By subtly mimicking them, they are showing that they're in sync with them. These are the lengths many will go to for that hard-earned promotion.

Done wrong and it won't impress. Their actions may become misinterpreted as questioning their boss's leadership skills. Their boss may think that they believe they can do a better job. Instead, it may be seen as an invasive communication method. If mirroring is done in an over-obvious manner, then they can kiss that promotion goodbye! Or, if they happen to mimic their boss's negative movements, such as if they lick their lips a lot, they will soon be out of favor. The boss might read this as a fun-poking process and feel offended. It's a fine line to walk.

Group Influences

If you want to influence someone in a group to agree with your point of view or new idea, watch out for who's doing the mirroring and who is being mirrored. That way you are identifying who has the authority to agree with you. The one being mirrored is clearly a person of interest.

If you can show that you feel confident through your body language to a room full of people, you will build up confidence in those around you. Those that can do this, often find themselves as the natural leader of any group. Though if you enter the room yawning and rubbing your eyes, you're more likely to put your audience to sleep.

You can tell from the body language of your audience whether they agree or disagree with what you are trying to convey. Those in disagreement may act a little differently to everyone else. They will look like the odd one out if you learn what signs to look for. Though you might need to focus, if they're good at it too, it may be very subtle.

We only tend to mirror each other when in conversation with people we know. It's unlikely we will mirror the behavior of complete strangers. It would not seem normal to mimic the person stood next to you in a queue for the cinema. Nor would we mimic people we're not very impressed with. It appears that mirroring has a hierarchy. Mimicking another's body language is a powerful tool for nonverbal communication. Not only can it help with that promotion, but it can also reveal whether someone has romantic intentions.

Chapter 14 Dress Code Language

The messages you give away are not only through the use of your body language. Another form of nonverbal secrets can be how we wear and use our clothing and accessories. Our clothes are a part of our body, a kind of outer skin. There are few people who consider walking around naked to be the norm. Nor would we wear our pajamas to go to work or a business suit to bed.

We have discussed how the first few seconds of meeting someone can often be crucial to how we perceive them. For a part of that critical assessment, we will also be considering their visual presentation. Our judgment will include how a person looks, as well as how they move. We do all that before they mutter a single word.

It all comes back to that tiny window of our first impression. If we want to impress someone, we must wear what makes us feel good. When we dress up to go on a special night out, we can feel like we're walking on air. It's not only about attraction, but it's also about our identity. Visual identity is yet another unwritten set of rules sending out a message about who we are. Our clothing and accessories can also give away our social status in life. We advertise how financially comfortable we are and show our cultural background. Even our age and sexual identity can be reflected in our choice of dress. The clothes on your back are a powerful tool in nonverbal communication.

To emphasize this, let's consider some different forms of dress:

- Loose ill-fitting clothes that appear grubby, may give off the impression that the person is lazy and maybe even unhygienic.
- In Western cultures, if a woman wears a low-cut neckline on a tight dress, it may give off the impression her out for fun and seeking a sexual encounter.
- A man in a suit could be a businessman, or someone attending a formal occasion.

- Yet, if he wore open-toed sandals with his business suit it would certainly draw attention. It would confuse, as no one would expect these two pieces of clothing to go together.

What we wear clearly sends out a strong message but so too does our grooming. Many of us are fixated on how we look. Women paint in eyebrows to look attractive. Men hate it when their hair begins to thin-out on their head as it advertises aging. Are we a vain species or is this all simply a part of our communication methods?

If we are interviewing for employment, we like to look the part and dress in formal wear. We're attempting to give off a good impression which may help us to be the successful candidate. Not only has that, dressing-up helped to boost our confidence. Our clothing is our identity costume.

If we want to show respect to others, then we usually

dress according to the unwritten rules. If we don't follow those rules then we give off a message of being deviant.

Nonverbal movements can send different messages for different cultures, so too can our costume of clothing:

- In the Middle East, a woman may feel quite vulnerable if she does not wear a burqa. Though because it's a warm clime she could walk around barefoot and no one would give a second glance.
- Yet, if you were to walk around barefoot in a Western city, people would think you rather odd. Nor would a woman need to cover her head with a burqa.

Most of us are practical and want to feel comfortable, so we tend to wear the right style of clothing for the occasion. There's no denying that what you wear sends out a loud visual message. If you are going to wear flashy clothes, then you'd better have the demeanor to match or others may be suspicious of you. Many of us wear what we can afford to buy. So it seems a little unfair and judgmental that so much is read into what a person is wearing.

It's not only clothing but your accessories too, particularly for women. These are not necessary items of clothing so if you choose to wear them, think about what they say about you. Plus, the perfumes we use, the way we wear our hair, the list is endless on how others might judge us.

Think of it this way, if we all dressed identically, we would lose an important tool that helps us to assess one another. Life would be rather boring if we all had the same personality, and equally if we all wore the same clothes.

In reality, we shouldn't put so much weight behind what someone is wearing. We should take the time to learn more instead of brushing over the surface. When assessing new people, we should all be a little more patient and a little less judgmental.

How then can we decide if we can trust someone and welcome them, if not by first impressions?

Chapter 15 Making Friends Without Speaking A Word

Charisma

Some people seemingly have the ability to walk into a room and instantly turn heads. They ooze in charisma and have everyone's attention even before they mutter a single word. These people seem to be born leaders, the alphas, or the top dogs.

How did they learn to be so popular?

One thing for certain, we are not born charismatic so it must be something we can all learn to do.

One standout attribute of those who are charismatic is that they exude confidence. Their body language will play an important role in maintaining that popularity. Having an open and approachable body stance plays a key role in being popular and making friends. Your openness should invite friendliness but not display weakness. Though we all have weaknesses, we must learn to hide them well. Essentially, that smile you show off must look authentic and not false.

A charismatic person is always a good listener, or at least they should look as though they are. It's all about a pleasant attitude and giving substance and value to your words and movements. Inspiring others and compelling them to act. Remember, nonverbal movements reflect emotional moods. If you keep your head clear and focus on the show of confident words and movements, you should at least look the part.

Not everyone has that natural feeling of warmth towards other people. But you can learn how to feel relaxed when in other people's company. Focus on the other people and take your mind away from your own emotions. Get your mind in sync with your body movements. If you have practiced relaxation techniques, this will shine through in your attitude and movement.

It's much like the natural smile that releases endorphins. Stand tall and you will feel tall.

If you see someone slouching in a chair, what is your first impression of them? You're likely to sweep your eyes right past them because they make no significant impact upon you. You may even think they're drunk or tired and so not worth any attention.

Try to treat everyone as though you are about to make them your personal friend. What then is the right way to go about making friends?

Friendships And Acquaintances

It isn't easy to make someone so at ease that they feel like they've known you a lifetime. Having the skill to do that though will no doubt foster new friendships. The important point is that it is not words alone that help you achieve this but your reactions.

They are already subconsciously scanning your body language. Now's the time be making that first impression count. Although we know we should not judge with so little information at hand, the fact is that we do. It isn't a conscious decision as we do it without even thinking about it. If you want to learn better communication skills, then make it your new life goal to do gestures consciously. Greet strangers with a warm smile. Make it a genuine one so that it reflects through your eyes and facial muscles.

Oculesics - Eye Contact

Grab their attention with eye to eye contact. The average time we look at each other is only a mere 10-seconds, so make the most of it. Maintaining eye contact, even if the other looks away, is vital to allow your own confidence to shine through. Though tread carefully and don't overdo it. That could be seen as a challenge, which wouldn't get your first meeting off to a good start.

As you introduce yourself, observe how they are reacting. For example, if they don't maintain eye contact, it may imply they lack confidence themselves. It's up to you to make them feel comfortable and therefore more confident in your company.

Haptics – The Power Of Touch

If you must share a handshake, take their whole hand in a firm grasp. Don't act as if you think they have some disease and you don't wish to touch them for too long. Wait until they let go, allowing them to take the lead. Of course, don't make it so firm that it's seen as aggressive. Shaking their arm out of their socket will not achieve the positive reaction you seek.

Try a handshake with both hands if they appear to be nervous or lacking in confidence. Gently place your other hand on top of theirs, completely encompassing it.

This type of touch-communication is known as Haptics. It is often reserved for those you love and trust. What you are doing is showing them that you are not afraid to do something out of the ordinary. Especially if it means you can help them to feel more at ease. If done in the correct manner, you will come across as warm and open-minded.

Listen And Mirror

To understand another's movements, it's wise to keep your own nonverbal actions open, wide open. Listen to their words and observe their movements closely. Only then can you react correctly, even to point of mirroring. If they smile, return it with a warm open smile.

Resist any urge to fold any parts of your body, even if the other person does this. Be the leader and show an openness that reflects your honesty. That way they may begin to mirror you and you can be confident you have helped them to relax.

Proxemics – Space

Focus on how far apart you position yourself from the person you are speaking with. Don't enter their personal space, but don't be too far away that they have to raise their voice to be heard.

You should be conscious of your movements as you talk. This will be hard work as it goes against the grain of subconsciously reflecting your own emotions. Push aside those emotions for a short while. Convince yourself that you like the person you are communicating with. Do this even if you don't, or if they are strangers. That way your body language will stay open and loose. You never know, it may lead to a lifelong friendship or an important working acquaintance.

Chapter 16 Nonverbal Socializing

Social Groups

If we're capable of changing how others perceive us, does that mean we can make friends easier? Humans are also social creatures, so it's good to build up a circle of trustworthy friends and acquaintances.

Anthropologist, Robin Dunbar, studied apes whilst they interacted in social group settings. He was able to determine how many individuals were close in the group, such as grooming buddies, by the size of their neocortex of the brain. Chimps, for instance, have a social circle of around 50, but only 2 or 3 grooming friends. Humans have a larger neocortex than apes and chimps. So, by extrapolating the research, he surmised that we can maintain an outer social group of up to 150 people. Though, like the chimps, that number falls for close friendships to around 12 people. Another difference is that humans use language to bond, unlike chimps who use grooming.

It shows that our means of communicating enables us to build up larger social networks. There's nothing worse than having a false group of friends. People who let us down when we need them. Improve your communications skills to better understand body language. Then, you can then choose your friends wisely.

Manipulation In The Nicest Possible Way

Reading nonverbal movements that reveal a person's inner thoughts, is a powerful tool. In a sense, you can manipulate how other people perceive you, via your body language.

If we like a person we've met, not necessarily in a romantic way, we try harder to impress them. To make the correct judgments we need to understand more about their personality. By paying close attention to nonverbal reactions, it gives us the advantage to make the right choices.

This is a time when eye contact is important. If the other person averts their gaze from yours, then they're either not interested or they're a little shy. If you continue to use your improved communication skills, you can delve a little deeper and work out which reason it is

Use open body language to show that you have nothing to hide. Don't make rash or unexpected moves. It's far better to take your time with movements. No fidgeting or nervous twitches. Be transparent so other people get the impression that you're confident and in control. Don't over gesticulate when you speak. Keep your arms low and your movements slow. A calm controlled approach will help you come across as someone in control.

Continue to use that warm smile on and off so you appear friendly. If you feel the smile, you'll make yourself feel better too and this will come across as warm and inviting.

It's not all about the body language either. Monitor your own words, for example, when offering to buy the other person a drink, don't make it sound as if you're doing them a favor. Instead, make it sound like a friendly gesture, such as: "I'm about to order a drink, would you like one?"

With this approach, you are showing your willingness to "share." You are asking if they'd like to join you. If your body language is open as well, then you will be setting a relaxed scene as best you can. If they agree, this is your cue to shift a little bit closer into their personal space. Tread carefully because too much too soon could send the encounter into a downward spiral.

If a conversation ensues, make sure you listen to their words and respond to them with your body. Nodding your head in the right places is a good start. You have the advantage because you know that they will be watching your movements subconsciously. Lean closer towards them if you can. This is another gesture that you are taking an interest in what they have to say.

Another tactic is to mirror their movements but don't be too obvious. If they tilt their head, tilt yours a little too. Don't overdo it though, this is a fine line you are learning to walk.

The importance of mirroring can be seen in a study from 2008 [19]. Using students in a negotiating situation, those who mirrored were successful in the test 67% of the time. Those who were not mirroring were only successful 12.5% of the time.

Once you feel the connection between, you can easily identify their mirroring of your actions. Try a yawn as this always works. Now you have a topic of humor to discuss, "erm...I think we both missed out on sleep last night, what's your story?" As they respond, lean in closer to listen to their words.

If they close up in their posture, such as crossing their arms or turning the top half of their body away, don't mirror. Such negative movements won't look good. You need to get the other person to relax. Show them your vulnerable regions, such as tilting your head back a little to expose your throat. Open up your hands and show your palms. By exposing yourself this way you are opening up to them.

By being observant and mirroring their behavior, you are putting yourself in sync with the other person. This will help to build up a rapport so you can identify with each other. If you can get in sync, you can pace the meeting on equal grounds. Whilst you're both evaluating each other, it is you who can lead the way. That's because you've taken the time to have a better understanding of the nonverbal clues. If you want a relationship to work, then bring out the best in yourself and the best in the other person.

Chapter 17 Improve Your Own Communication Skills

Does it come down to how we perceive one another's nonverbal gestures or is it more complex than that?

For most of us, it's true to say that we don't even think about how we interpret other people's body language, nor they ours. Unless you come across a guide such as this one, or a media article on the topic. That's because it's something that we do automatically.

Given that no one's taking notes, imagine if you could manipulate your body language to send out the wrong messages. The art of any sales representative proves how persuasive body language can be. If you can learn to manipulate others by using nonverbal signals, it would certainly lend you an advantage. Just as you can tell lies with verbal words, so too you can mislead others with nonverbal messages.

Benefits

Improving your communication skills is not about misleading others, although some may use it for that. Instead, it's about using these skills to become a better person. It's about understanding your own, and other people's, subconscious thoughts.

By communicating more effectively, you could potentially:

- Advance your career prospects to improve your lifestyle.
- Boost your confidence, by learning power poses using nonverbal actions.
- Increase your popularity, by learning to show how interested you are in listening.
- Get others to agree with you, by eliminating nonverbal barriers and being more open.
- Make others feel better about themselves, by stimulating their mood.
- Recognize the truth from an outright mistruth.

Is all this achievable without using one word?

Of course, we still need words otherwise we would not have developed languages. It's important though to make sure the verbal language matches the nonverbal communication. If it doesn't, then all you will succeed in doing is causing confusion.

It's a skill that takes some understanding, interpreting and patience. To use a person's movements to your advantage, you must learn to decipher nonverbal messages correctly. To do this it's essential that you research and re-teach yourself on the body language of your own culture. Be aware of the multiple meanings of some gestures, such as arm crossing. Does the situation mean it's a defensive posture for the subject, or are they cold?

Other Skills To Improve

Be a good listener. Lean in and make sure your pose is open. Don't become distracted when having a conversation. Repeat things back to the other person to make sure you understood the message they are communicating to you. You should work on never controlling a conversation. Instead, actively listen. Then, what you give back will contribute to the quality of the dialogue.

Don't be judgmental. No scowling or crossing of any of your own body parts. Negative movements will make the other person feel uneasy. This is about improving your own thoughts too. It's important to work at having an open mind to all things. If you hear something you don't like, explore it further without judgment. Show more interest in the topic so you can better understand where the other person is coming from.

Learn the meanings behind nonverbal movements so you can decipher other people's emotions. This will be a great skill to have, helping you to improve your own empathy of people and the problems in their lives.

When someone is verbally telling you about their experiences, don't come back at them with your own. Watch their nonverbal movements to understand their mood. Is it a sad tale that upsets them, embarrasses them, or makes them feel bitter or angry? By learning to pick up on their emotions, you are far better placed to help them. This is far more beneficial than simply comparing your own experiences to them.

Don't contradict people when you disagree with them. In general, it means they will have to retaliate and that may damage your relationship. We all love a good debate, and that's fine if that's what you're having. Free yourself of your own ego by not thinking about your own opinions and experiences all the time.

Don't forget that warm smile, use it, a lot, but make sure it's in the right context. Make it a slow smile so the rest of your face looks expressive. It will get those facial muscles in alignment and look more authentic.

Angle your chin downwards a little so you don't come over as if you're looking down your nose at someone.

Show your palms, it helps to make you appear open and approachable. This will put others at ease.

Dealing With Another's Deviant Tactics

Don't give them much of your time. They are clearly wanting something from you, so ask them outright what they want. Watch their body language so you can work out their misleading code. They may be very apt at the same communications game that you yourself are trying to learn, only for different reasons. There's no need to be aggressive. You could even congratulate them on their amazing communication skills. Then challenge their motives face-to-face, keeping the mood light.

Dealing With Your Own Interpretations

It's a tall order when you set about learning any new skill. For this one, you already have the tools in place. You've been using this method of communicating all your life. All you need to do now is to become more observant of others, and more aware of your own movements too.

It can be a daunting task trying to improve these skills. The hardest part is interpreting which postures and movements fit within the situation. As we have seen, many body movements can have different meanings in different situations.

Once again, think of the folding arms example.

- Is it cold?
- Are they bored?
- Are they putting up a barrier?
- Watch for those facial features to confirm why the person is shutting you off.

- What is the rest of the body telling you?
- How are you going to help this person change their mind and relax?

Another example is that smile.

- Are they smiling yet looking down at the floor?
- Are they putting on a brave smile while tears roll down their cheeks?
- Is that smile in the eyes and the rest of the facial muscles?

Or, what about that powerful handshake?

- A weaker one does not necessarily mean they are weak-minded. Do they have a hand injury or arthritis?

As you can see, it's not only about observing body language but also matching it up with the situation that you're in. Remember that what you're really reading is the other person's emotions. A set of feelings that can be very complex to read. Get it wrong and you could add fuel to fire, or at best you could end up embarrassing yourself.

It's also about combining their movements with the voice that they're using. What is the tone and pitch of their words?

There are so many tiny little hitches you need to be aware of. Such as, when using eye contact to build up a good rapport, do it in small intervals. Experts recommend only 4-5-second intervals, then move your eyes away to give the other person a break. The last thing you want to end up doing is having a staring competition.

Progressive Stages

The first rule has to be "practice." As with most new skills, the more you do it over and over, the better you become.

The better you become, the more people will find you interesting and want to associate with you, so long as you are using it positively.

Don't use this powerful skill to manipulate people or you may become very unpopular, or even labeled as a bully.

The more popular you become as your confidence increases, the more likely others will see you as a useful person. We all love to be liked and that in itself should be your reward.

Be more honest and open and you might just:

- Gain that promotion.
- Make new friends and acquaintances.
- Get those sales figures on an upward trend.

Best of all, become a better person.

Conclusion

This guide should open your mind to a daily process that we all take for granted. Our nonverbal communications. When you find out how much information you are signaling, without even realizing it, you will see how important it is to disguise those clues. Most especially if you desire to be successful in your life.

Interpreting someone else's complex body language is not easy. You will need to identify some of the small, almost invisible, movements we have written about. Then, you must try and fit them according to the situation you are in.

Whether at a business meeting or a romantic liaison, you can learn to read between the lines of what people are saying. It takes a good deal of practice to make sure you don't misinterpret what you're observing. So, don't think you can learn this skill overnight.

Once you feel confident that you're reading the right messages, you can then begin controlling your own nonverbal signals. Make sure you always come across as confident and clear, by knowing what to give away and what not to make so obvious.

If you're intrigued by the mysteries of body language, then you're not alone. It's only one small part of the intricacies of communication between people. Our ability to feel so many emotions is what makes humans such a convoluted species. This is a small part of understanding what we're all about. If you can master the secrets of nonverbal communications, you will get to know other people better than they know themselves.

As you become more aware of the people around you, business associates or your social circle, you will be better able to help them. That's because you can read when they have conflicting emotions. If you've read this book through, and taken in the advice and techniques we have shown you, then you'll know to do.

Whilst we think our verbal words instruct others on what we wish to communicate, they only cover a small part of our message. Emotions are not conveyed in a verbal language unless we chose to do so. Yet, in nonverbal communications, we give our emotions away without knowing it. Once you can comprehend that, then, and only then, will you get the full picture of what people are expressing. They do this every day, so you have a lot to learn and understand.

Use this guide to improve your own communication skills. Better understand what others communicate with their movements, that they're not saying with their words. You might find one or two surprises within these pages. Use them as a guide to make you a better person for this new skill. We all have room for improvement, so long as we never stop learning.

References

1. When you smile, the world smiles at you: ERP evidence for self-expression effects on face processing Social Cognitive and Affective Neuroscience, Volume 10, Issue 10, 1 October 2015, Pages 1316–1322 Alejandra Sel Beatriz Calvo-Merino, Simone Tuettenberg, Bettina Forster

2. https://pure.mpg.de/rest/items/item_2309885/com ponent/file_2309884/content Darwin C. (1872) 'The expression of the emotions in man and animals"

3. 'Constants across cultures in the face and emotion' Journal of Personality and Social Psychology 1971, Vol. 17, No. 2, 124-129 Ekman P. Friesen WV (1971) W. V. O'Sullivan, M. Chan, A. Diacoyanni-Tarlatzis, I. Heider, K. Tzavaras, (1987). Universals and cultural differences in the judgments of facial expressions of

emotion. Journal of Personality and Social Psychology, 53(4), 712-717

4. Attard-Johnson J, Bindemann M (2017) 'Sex-specific but not sexually explicit: pupillary responses to dressed and naked adults' The Royal Society Open Science Attard-Johnson J, Bindemann M (2017)

5. https://www.iasj.net/iasj?func=fulltext&aId=73926 Mayada R. Eesa Assistant Lecturer Ministry of Higher Education and Scientific Research Facial Expressions A study of Eyebrow Movement During Conversation. chapter 3.1

6. https://www.newswise.com/articles/gestures-fulfill-a-role-in-language Accoustal Society of America (ASA) "Gestures fulfil a role in language." Article ID: 589058 8-May-2012

7. Dinica R.C. (2014) 'Non-verbal communication - indispensable complement of oral and written communication' Procedia - Social and Behavioral Sciences 137 (2014) 105 – 111

8. South Palomares, J. K. and Young, A. W. (2018) 'Facial First Impressions of Partner Preference Traits: Trustworthiness, Status, and Attractiveness', Social Psychological and Personality Science, 9, pp. 990–1000.

9. https://doi.org/10.1177/0956797614532474 Todorov, A., & Porter, J. M. (2014). Misleading First Impressions: Different for Different Facial Images of the Same Person. Psychological Science, 25(7), 1404–1417.

10. doi:10.1525/aa.1963.65.5.02a00020

11. Edward T. Hall (1963). "A System for the Notation of Proxemic Behaviour." American Anthropologist. 65 (5): 1003–1026.

12. https://doi.org/10.1523/JNEUROSCI.0686-13.2014 (100): Daphne J. Holt, Brittany S. Cassidy, Xiaomin Yue, Scott L. Rauch, Emily A. Boeke, Shahin Nasr, Roger B. H. Tootell and Garth Coombs (2014) 'Neural Correlates of Personal Space Intrusion' Journal of Neuroscience 19 March 2014

13. DePaulo, B. M., Lindsay, J. J., Malone, B. E., Muhlenbruck, L., Charlton, K., & Cooper, H. (2003). Cues to deception. Psychological Bulletin, 129, 74–118

14. Eckman, p., Frieson W.V., Depaulo B.M., (2006) 'Accuracy of Deception Judgments' Personality and Social Psychology Review 2006, Vol. 10, No. 3, 214–234

15. 'Social Influence Stel, M., & Dijk E., (2018) 'When do we see that others misrepresent how they feel? Detecting deception from emotional faces with direct and indirect measures. Volume 13, 2018 - Issue 3

16. ten Brinke, L., Stimson, D. and Carney, D. R. (2014) 'Some Evidence for Unconscious Lie Detection', Psychological Science, 25(5), pp. 1098–1105. doi: 10.1177/0956797614524421.

17. Mehrabian, A. (1981). Silent messages: Implicit communication of emotions and attitudes. Belmont, CA: Wadsworth

18. Réale D, Reader SM, Sol D, McDougall PT, Dingemanse NJ (2007) 'Integrating animal temperament within ecology and evolution.' Biol Rev Camb Philos Soc. 2007 May;82(2):291-318.

19. W. Allport, Gordon & E. Vernon, Philip. (1933). Studies in Expressive Movement. 10.1037/11566-000

20. https://digitalcommons.butler.edu/cgi/viewcontent.cgi?article=1045&context=cob_papers   McQuiston D.H., Morris, K.A., (2009) 'Gender Differences In Communication: Implications For Salespeople' Butler University Scholarship and Professional Work - Business

21. https://anthrosource.onlinelibrary.wiley.com/doi/abs/10.1525/aa.1966.68.4.02a00070   Quantitative Research in Proxemic Behavior O. MICHAEL WATSON: THEODORE D. GRAVES First published: August 1966

22. Ekman, P., & Friesen, W. (1971).' Constants across culture in the face and emotion.' Journal of Personality and Social Psychology, 17, 124–129

23. https://doi.org/10.1371/journal.pone.0173942

McDuff D., Kodra E., el Kailouby R. LaFrance, M. (2017) 'A large-scale analysis of sex differences in facial expressions' PloSOne, 12(4), e0173942.

Disclaimer

The information contained in this book and its components, is meant to serve as a comprehensive collection of strategies that the author of this book has done research about. Summaries, strategies, tips and tricks are only recommendations by the author, and reading this book will not guarantee that one's results will exactly mirror the author's results.

The author of this book has made all reasonable efforts to provide current and accurate information for the readers of this book. The author and its associates will not be held liable for any unintentional errors or omissions that may be found.

The material in the book may include information by third-parties. Third-party materials comprise of opinions expressed by their owners. As such, the author of this book does not assume responsibility or liability for any third-party material or opinions.

written expressed and signed permission from the author.

Printed in Great Britain
by Amazon